POD
Upload & Update Log
Indie Book Management

Book # _____

From: _____ to _____

WestWard Journals
WestWard Books
Payson, Arizona

WestWard Journals

Copyright © 2018 Marsha Ward
WestWard Books

Cover Photo by Annie Spratt on Unsplash

ISBN-13: 978-1-947306-09-7

INTRODUCTION

This Log contains space to make note of upload and update details for six self-published print books. It is intended to be used for books printed by KDP Print, but probably is flexible enough for other POD services, too. It contains ample pages for notes about updates and changes, which should help keep track of any details the Indie or Self-Publishing Author and Publisher may need.

MY PROJECT IDEAS

_____

_____

_____

_____

_____

_____

_____

_____

_____

_____

_____

_____

_____

_____

_____

_____

_____

_____

_____

_____

_____

_____

MY BOOKS

Book 1   Title _____   Page 1
_____
_____

Book 2   Title _____   Page 9
_____
_____

Book 3   Title _____   Page 17
_____
_____

Book 4   Title _____   Page 25
_____
_____

Book 5   Title _____   Page 33
_____
_____

Book 6   Title _____   Page 41
_____
_____

MORE PROJECT IDEAS

BOOK 1 - Date _____

Paperback Details

Language _____

Book Title _____

Subtitle _____

Series _____ # _____

Edition Number (if it applies) _____

Author _____

Contributors (if any) _____

_____

_____

_____

Description: _____

_____

_____

_____

_____

_____

_____

_____

_____

_____

_____

_____

_____

Publishing Rights (circle or underline one)

        I own the copyright

        This is a public domain work

Book Title _____

Keywords (seven words or phrases)

_____

_____

_____

_____

_____

_____

_____

Categories (two)

_____

_____

_____

_____

Large Print	No	Yes
Adult Content	No	Yes

Paperback Content

Print ISBN (circle one)　　Free KDP　My Own

ISBN _____

Imprint _____

Publication Date _____

Print Options circle one

Black & white interior with cream paper

Black & white interior with white paper

Color interior with white paper

Trim Size chosen: _____

Book Title _____

    Bleed settings   No Bleed Bleed

    Paperback cover finish (circle one)   Matte Glossy

Manuscript

    File name _____

    Uploaded   Date _____

    Updated   Date _____

    Updated   Date _____

    Updated   Date _____

    Interior Formatter _____

    Contact Info: _____

    Cost: _____

Book Cover

    File name _____

    Uploaded   Date _____

    Updated   Date _____

    Updated   Date _____

    Updated   Date _____

    Cover Designer _____

    Contact Info: _____

    Cost: _____

Book Preview - Approved Date _____

    Downloaded a PDF Proof   Date _____

Summary

    Page Count _____ Your Printing Cost _____

    Notes _____

    _____

Book Title _____

Paperback Rights & Pricing

Territories (circle one)

    All territories

    Individual territories

_____

_____

_____

_____

_____

_____

Pricing & Royalty

    Primary Marketplace _____

    List Price Chosen _____ Currency _____

    Rate _____ Printing _____ Royalty _____

    Expanded Distribution?   Yes   No

    * Other Marketplace _____

    List Price Chosen _____ Currency _____

    Rate _____ Printing _____ Royalty _____

    * Other Marketplace _____

    List Price Chosen _____ Currency _____

    Rate _____ Printing _____ Royalty _____

    * Other Marketplace _____

    List Price Chosen _____ Currency _____

    Rate _____ Printing _____ Royalty _____

Book Title _____

    * Other Marketplace _____

    List Price Chosen _____ Currency _____

    Rate _____ Printing _____ Royalty _____

    * Other Marketplace _____

    List Price Chosen _____ Currency _____

    Rate _____ Printing _____ Royalty _____

    * Other Marketplace _____

    List Price Chosen _____ Currency _____

    Rate _____ Printing _____ Royalty _____

Proof Copies

    Requested a proof copy   Date _____

    Arrival Date _____

Publication Status

    Saved as Draft Date _____

    Clicked Publish Button Date _____

    Published Notice from KDP Date _____

    Notes _____

    _____

    _____

    _____

    _____

    _____

    _____

    _____

Book Title _____

Author Copy Orders

Date	#	Ship Speed	Ship Cost	Tax	Total	Arrived

Book Title _____

Note Date & Changes Made

_____

_____

_____

_____

_____

_____

_____

_____

_____

_____

_____

_____

_____

_____

_____

_____

_____

_____

_____

_____

_____

_____

_____

_____

_____

_____

_____

_____

_____

_____

_____

Book Title _____

Note Date & Changes Made

_____
_____
_____
_____
_____
_____
_____
_____
_____
_____
_____
_____
_____
_____
_____
_____
_____
_____
_____
_____
_____
_____
_____
_____
_____
_____
_____
_____
_____
_____

BOOK 2 - Date _____

Paperback Details

Language _____

Book Title _____

Subtitle _____

Series _____ # _____

Edition Number (if it applies) _____

Author _____

Contributors (if any) _____

_____

_____

_____

Description: _____

_____

_____

_____

_____

_____

_____

_____

_____

_____

_____

_____

Publishing Rights (circle or underline one)

      I own the copyright

      This is a public domain work

Book Title _____

Keywords (seven words or phrases)

_____

_____

_____

_____

_____

_____

_____

Categories (two)

_____

_____

_____

_____

| Large Print | No | Yes |
| Adult Content | No | Yes |

Paperback Content

Print ISBN (circle one)   Free KDP   My Own

   ISBN _____

   Imprint _____

   Publication Date _____

Print Options circle one

   Black & white interior with cream paper

   Black & white interior with white paper

   Color interior with white paper

   Trim Size chosen: _____

Book Title _____

    Bleed settings   No Bleed Bleed

    Paperback cover finish (circle one)   Matte Glossy

Manuscript

    File name _____

    Uploaded   Date _____

    Updated   Date _____

    Updated   Date _____

    Updated   Date _____

    Interior Formatter _____

    Contact Info: _____

    Cost: _____

Book Cover

    File name _____

    Uploaded   Date _____

    Updated   Date _____

    Updated   Date _____

    Updated   Date _____

    Cover Designer _____

    Contact Info: _____

    Cost: _____

Book Preview - Approved Date _____

    Downloaded a PDF Proof   Date _____

Summary

    Page Count _____ Your Printing Cost _____

    Notes _____

    _____

Book Title _____

Paperback Rights & Pricing

Territories (circle one)

    All territories

    Individual territories

_____

_____

_____

_____

_____

_____

Pricing & Royalty

    Primary Marketplace _____

    List Price Chosen _____ Currency ____

    Rate _____ Printing _____ Royalty _____

    Expanded Distribution?   Yes   No

    * Other Marketplace _____

    List Price Chosen _____ Currency ____

    Rate _____ Printing _____ Royalty _____

    * Other Marketplace _____

    List Price Chosen _____ Currency ____

    Rate _____ Printing _____ Royalty _____

    * Other Marketplace _____

    List Price Chosen _____ Currency ____

    Rate _____ Printing _____ Royalty _____

Book Title _____

    * Other Marketplace _____

    List Price Chosen _____ Currency ____

    Rate _____ Printing _____ Royalty _____

    * Other Marketplace _____

    List Price Chosen _____ Currency ____

    Rate _____ Printing _____ Royalty _____

    * Other Marketplace _____

    List Price Chosen _____ Currency ____

    Rate _____ Printing _____ Royalty _____

Proof Copies

    Requested a proof copy   Date _____

    Arrival Date _____

Publication Status

    Saved as Draft Date _____

    Clicked Publish Button Date _____

    Published Notice from KDP Date _____

    Notes _____

    _____

    _____

    _____

    _____

    _____

    _____

    _____

Book Title _____

Author Copy Orders

Date	#	Ship Speed	Ship Cost	Tax	Total	Arrived

Book Title _____

Note Date & Changes Made

_____
_____
_____
_____
_____
_____
_____
_____
_____
_____
_____
_____
_____
_____
_____
_____
_____
_____
_____
_____
_____
_____
_____
_____
_____
_____
_____

Book Title _____

Note Date & Changes Made

_____

_____

_____

_____

_____

_____

_____

_____

_____

_____

_____

_____

_____

_____

_____

_____

_____

_____

_____

_____

_____

_____

_____

_____

_____

_____

_____

_____

BOOK 3 - Date _____

Paperback Details

Language _____

Book Title _____

Subtitle _____

Series _____ # _____

Edition Number (if it applies) _____

Author _____

Contributors (if any) _____

_____

_____

_____

Description: _____

_____

_____

_____

_____

_____

_____

_____

_____

_____

_____

_____

_____

_____

Publishing Rights (circle or underline one)

      I own the copyright

      This is a public domain work

Book Title _____

Keywords (seven words or phrases)

_____

_____

_____

_____

_____

_____

_____

Categories (two)

_____

_____

_____

| Large Print | No | Yes |
| Adult Content | No | Yes |

Paperback Content

Print ISBN (circle one)   Free KDP   My Own

   ISBN _____

   Imprint _____

   Publication Date _____

Print Options circle one

   Black & white interior with cream paper

   Black & white interior with white paper

   Color interior with white paper

   Trim Size chosen: _____

Book Title _____

      Bleed settings   No Bleed   Bleed

      Paperback cover finish (circle one)   Matte   Glossy

Manuscript

      File name _____

      Uploaded   Date _____

      Updated   Date _____

      Updated   Date _____

      Updated   Date _____

      Interior Formatter _____

      Contact Info: _____

      Cost: _____

Book Cover

      File name _____

      Uploaded   Date _____

      Updated   Date _____

      Updated   Date _____

      Updated   Date _____

      Cover Designer _____

      Contact Info: _____

      Cost: _____

Book Preview - Approved Date _____

      Downloaded a PDF Proof   Date _____

Summary

      Page Count _____ Your Printing Cost _____

      Notes _____

      _____

Book Title _____

Paperback Rights & Pricing

Territories (circle one)

    All territories

    Individual territories

_____

_____

_____

_____

_____

_____

Pricing & Royalty

    Primary Marketplace _____

    List Price Chosen _____ Currency _____

    Rate _____ Printing _____ Royalty _____

    Expanded Distribution?   Yes   No

    * Other Marketplace _____

    List Price Chosen _____ Currency _____

    Rate _____ Printing _____ Royalty _____

    * Other Marketplace _____

    List Price Chosen _____ Currency _____

    Rate _____ Printing _____ Royalty _____

    * Other Marketplace _____

    List Price Chosen _____ Currency _____

    Rate _____ Printing _____ Royalty _____

Book Title _____

* Other Marketplace _____

List Price Chosen _____ Currency _____

Rate _____ Printing _____ Royalty _____

* Other Marketplace _____

List Price Chosen _____ Currency _____

Rate _____ Printing _____ Royalty _____

* Other Marketplace _____

List Price Chosen _____ Currency _____

Rate _____ Printing _____ Royalty _____

Proof Copies

Requested a proof copy   Date _____

Arrival Date _____

Publication Status

Saved as Draft Date _____

Clicked Publish Button Date _____

Published Notice from KDP Date _____

Notes _____

_____

_____

_____

_____

_____

_____

_____

Book Title _____

Author Copy Orders

Date	#	Ship Speed	Ship Cost	Tax	Total	Arrived

Book Title _____

Note Date & Changes Made

_____

_____

_____

_____

_____

_____

_____

_____

_____

_____

_____

_____

_____

_____

_____

_____

_____

_____

_____

_____

_____

_____

_____

_____

_____

Book Title _____

Note Date & Changes Made

_____
_____
_____
_____
_____
_____
_____
_____
_____
_____
_____
_____
_____
_____
_____
_____
_____
_____
_____
_____
_____
_____
_____
_____
_____
_____

BOOK 4 - Date _____

Paperback Details

Language _____

Book Title _____

Subtitle _____

Series _____ # ____

Edition Number (if it applies) _____

Author _____

Contributors (if any) _____

_____

_____

_____

Description: _____

_____

_____

_____

_____

_____

_____

_____

_____

_____

_____

_____

_____

Publishing Rights (circle or underline one)

      I own the copyright

      This is a public domain work

Book Title _____

    Keywords (seven words or phrases)

    _____

    _____

    _____

    _____

    _____

    _____

    _____

    Categories (two)

    _____

    _____

    _____

Large Print	No	Yes
Adult Content	No	Yes

Paperback Content

Print ISBN (circle one)   Free KDP My Own

    ISBN _____

    Imprint _____

    Publication Date _____

Print Options circle one

    Black & white interior with cream paper

    Black & white interior with white paper

    Color interior with white paper

    Trim Size chosen: _____

Book Title _____

Bleed settings   No Bleed Bleed

Paperback cover finish (circle one)   Matte Glossy

Manuscript

File name _____

Uploaded   Date _____

Updated   Date _____

Updated   Date _____

Updated   Date _____

Interior Formatter _____

Contact Info: _____

Cost: _____

Book Cover

File name _____

Uploaded   Date _____

Updated   Date _____

Updated   Date _____

Updated   Date _____

Cover Designer _____

Contact Info: _____

Cost: _____

Book Preview - Approved Date _____

Downloaded a PDF Proof   Date _____

Summary

Page Count _____ Your Printing Cost _____

Notes _____

_____

Book Title _____

Paperback Rights & Pricing

Territories (circle one)

    All territories

    Individual territories

_____

_____

_____

_____

_____

_____

Pricing & Royalty

    Primary Marketplace _____

    List Price Chosen _____ Currency _____

    Rate _____ Printing _____ Royalty _____

    Expanded Distribution?   Yes   No

    * Other Marketplace _____

    List Price Chosen _____ Currency _____

    Rate _____ Printing _____ Royalty _____

    * Other Marketplace _____

    List Price Chosen _____ Currency _____

    Rate _____ Printing _____ Royalty _____

    * Other Marketplace _____

    List Price Chosen _____ Currency _____

    Rate _____ Printing _____ Royalty _____

Book Title _____

* Other Marketplace _____

List Price Chosen _____ Currency ____

Rate _____ Printing _____ Royalty _____

* Other Marketplace _____

List Price Chosen _____ Currency ____

Rate _____ Printing _____ Royalty _____

* Other Marketplace _____

List Price Chosen _____ Currency ____

Rate _____ Printing _____ Royalty _____

Proof Copies

Requested a proof copy   Date _____

Arrival Date _____

Publication Status

Saved as Draft Date _____

Clicked Publish Button Date _____

Published Notice from KDP Date _____

Notes _____

_____

_____

_____

_____

_____

_____

_____

Book Title _____

Author Copy Orders

Date   #   Ship Speed   Ship Cost   Tax   Total   Arrived

_____

_____

_____

_____

_____

_____

_____

_____

_____

_____

_____

_____

_____

_____

_____

_____

_____

_____

_____

_____

_____

Book Title _____

Note Date & Changes Made

Book Title _____

Note Date & Changes Made

_____

_____

_____

_____

_____

_____

_____

_____

_____

_____

_____

_____

_____

_____

_____

_____

_____

_____

_____

_____

_____

_____

_____

_____

_____

_____

_____

_____

BOOK 5 - Date _____

Paperback Details

Language _____

Book Title _____

Subtitle _____

Series _____ # _____

Edition Number (if it applies) _____

Author _____

Contributors (if any) _____

_____

_____

_____

Description: _____

_____

_____

_____

_____

_____

_____

_____

_____

_____

_____

_____

Publishing Rights (circle or underline one)

        I own the copyright

        This is a public domain work

Book Title _____

Keywords (seven words or phrases)

_____

_____

_____

_____

_____

_____

_____

Categories (two)

_____

_____

_____

Large Print	No	Yes
Adult Content	No	Yes

Paperback Content

Print ISBN (circle one)   Free KDP   My Own

ISBN _____

Imprint _____

Publication Date _____

Print Options circle one

Black & white interior with cream paper

Black & white interior with white paper

Color interior with white paper

Trim Size chosen: _____

Book Title _____

Bleed settings   No Bleed   Bleed

Paperback cover finish (circle one)   Matte   Glossy

Manuscript

File name _____

Uploaded   Date _____

Updated   Date _____

Updated   Date _____

Updated   Date _____

Interior Formatter _____

Contact Info: _____

Cost: _____

Book Cover

File name _____

Uploaded   Date _____

Updated   Date _____

Updated   Date _____

Updated   Date _____

Cover Designer _____

Contact Info: _____

Cost: _____

Book Preview - Approved Date _____

Downloaded a PDF Proof   Date _____

Summary

Page Count _____ Your Printing Cost _____

Notes _____

_____

Book Title _____

Paperback Rights & Pricing

Territories (circle one)

    All territories

    Individual territories

_____

_____

_____

_____

_____

_____

Pricing & Royalty

    Primary Marketplace _____

    List Price Chosen _____ Currency ____

    Rate _____ Printing _____ Royalty _____

    Expanded Distribution?   Yes   No

    * Other Marketplace _____

    List Price Chosen _____ Currency ____

    Rate _____ Printing _____ Royalty _____

    * Other Marketplace _____

    List Price Chosen _____ Currency ____

    Rate _____ Printing _____ Royalty _____

    * Other Marketplace _____

    List Price Chosen _____ Currency ____

    Rate _____ Printing _____ Royalty _____

Book Title _____

    * Other Marketplace _____

    List Price Chosen _____ Currency _____

    Rate _____ Printing _____ Royalty _____

    * Other Marketplace _____

    List Price Chosen _____ Currency _____

    Rate _____ Printing _____ Royalty _____

    * Other Marketplace _____

    List Price Chosen _____ Currency _____

    Rate _____ Printing _____ Royalty _____

Proof Copies

    Requested a proof copy   Date _____

    Arrival Date _____

Publication Status

    Saved as Draft Date _____

    Clicked Publish Button Date _____

    Published Notice from KDP Date _____

    Notes _____

    _____

    _____

    _____

    _____

    _____

    _____

    _____

Book Title _____

Author Copy Orders

Date	#	Ship Speed	Ship Cost	Tax	Total	Arrived

Book Title _____

Note Date & Changes Made

_____

_____

_____

_____

_____

_____

_____

_____

_____

_____

_____

_____

_____

_____

_____

_____

_____

_____

_____

_____

_____

_____

_____

_____

_____

_____

_____

_____

Book Title _____

Note Date & Changes Made

_____
_____
_____
_____
_____
_____
_____
_____
_____
_____
_____
_____
_____
_____
_____
_____
_____
_____
_____
_____
_____
_____
_____
_____
_____
_____
_____
_____

BOOK 6 - Date _____

Paperback Details

Language _____

Book Title _____

Subtitle _____

Series _____ # ____

Edition Number (if it applies) _____

Author _____

Contributors (if any) _____

_____

_____

_____

Description: _____

_____

_____

_____

_____

_____

_____

_____

_____

_____

_____

_____

_____

Publishing Rights (circle or underline one)

I own the copyright

This is a public domain work

Book Title _____

Keywords (seven words or phrases)

_____

_____

_____

_____

_____

_____

_____

Categories (two)

_____

_____

_____

_____

Large Print	No	Yes
Adult Content	No	Yes

Paperback Content

Print ISBN (circle one)   Free KDP   My Own

   ISBN _____

   Imprint _____

   Publication Date _____

Print Options circle one

   Black & white interior with cream paper

   Black & white interior with white paper

   Color interior with white paper

   Trim Size chosen: _____

Book Title _____

    Bleed settings   No Bleed Bleed

    Paperback cover finish (circle one)   Matte Glossy

Manuscript

    File name _____

    Uploaded   Date _____

    Updated   Date _____

    Updated   Date _____

    Updated   Date _____

    Interior Formatter _____

    Contact Info: _____

    Cost: _____

Book Cover

    File name _____

    Uploaded   Date _____

    Updated   Date _____

    Updated   Date _____

    Updated   Date _____

    Cover Designer _____

    Contact Info: _____

    Cost: _____

Book Preview - Approved Date _____

    Downloaded a PDF Proof   Date _____

Summary

    Page Count _____ Your Printing Cost _____

    Notes _____

    _____

Book Title _____

Paperback Rights & Pricing

Territories (circle one)

    All territories

    Individual territories

_____

_____

_____

_____

_____

_____

Pricing & Royalty

    Primary Marketplace _____

    List Price Chosen _____ Currency ____

    Rate _____ Printing _____ Royalty _____

    Expanded Distribution?   Yes   No

    * Other Marketplace _____

    List Price Chosen _____ Currency ____

    Rate _____ Printing _____ Royalty _____

    * Other Marketplace _____

    List Price Chosen _____ Currency ____

    Rate _____ Printing _____ Royalty _____

    * Other Marketplace _____

    List Price Chosen _____ Currency ____

    Rate _____ Printing _____ Royalty _____

Book Title _____

    * Other Marketplace _____

    List Price Chosen _____ Currency _____

    Rate _____ Printing _____ Royalty _____

    * Other Marketplace _____

    List Price Chosen _____ Currency _____

    Rate _____ Printing _____ Royalty _____

    * Other Marketplace _____

    List Price Chosen _____ Currency _____

    Rate _____ Printing _____ Royalty _____

Proof Copies

    Requested a proof copy   Date _____

    Arrival Date _____

Publication Status

    Saved as Draft Date _____

    Clicked Publish Button Date _____

    Published Notice from KDP Date _____

    Notes _____

    _____

    _____

    _____

    _____

    _____

    _____

    _____

Book Title _____

Author Copy Orders

Date	#	Ship Speed	Ship Cost	Tax	Total	Arrived

Book Title _____

Note Date & Changes Made

_____

_____

_____

_____

_____

_____

_____

_____

_____

_____

_____

_____

_____

_____

_____

_____

_____

_____

_____

_____

_____

_____

_____

_____

_____

_____

_____

Book Title _____

Note Date & Changes Made

_____

_____

_____

_____

_____

_____

_____

_____

_____

_____

_____

_____

_____

_____

_____

_____

_____

_____

_____

_____

_____

_____

_____

_____

_____

_____

_____

_____

About the Creator of
WestWard Journals

Marsha Ward writes authentic historical fiction, and nonfiction having to do with writing. Her novels include The Owen Family Saga series, the Shenandoah Neighbors series, and many other works of fiction. Her nonfiction books include *The Checklist: Indie Publishing My Way, Rapid Recipes for Writers . . . And Other Busy People,* and *From Julia's Kitchen: Owen Family Cookery.*

Find her online at Amazon or at marshaward.com.

www.ingramcontent.com/pod-product-compliance
Lightning Source LLC
Chambersburg PA
CBHW060644280326
41933CB00012B/2150